S0-ACT-655

Everything I Know as a CEO
I Learned as a Waitress

12 Principles to Empower Your Life

By

Carolyn J. Gable

With
Mark Graham

Illustrations by Nick Galifianakis

It's All Good
Publishing, LLC
Lake Zurich, Illinois

Everything I Know as a CEO I Learned as a Waitress

12 Principles to Empower Your Life

© 2007 by Carolyn J. Gable, Lake Zurich, Illinois

Mark Graham of Denver, assisting

Illustrations by Nick Galifianakis of Falls Church, Virginia

All rights reserved.

FIRST EDITION

Printed in the United States of America

It's All Good Publishing, LLC
1881 Rose Road
Lake Zurich, IL 60047
847-545-1894
www.CarolynGable.com

Designed and produced by Chauncey Park Press,
735 N. Grove Avenue, Oak Park. Illinois 60302-1551 USA
708-524-0695 www.chaunceyparkpress.com

Printed on #60 Williamsburg Offset Text by International Paper.
Text and headlines set in Caslon.

Library of Congress Control Number: 2007922640

ISBN: 978-0-9793375-0-5 (Paperback)

1. Interpersonal Relations.   2. Self-Help Techniques

3. Expect a Miracle Foundation

Dedication

This book is dedicated to my seven children:
Ryan, Seth, Justin, Whitney, Jake, Luke, and Ava.
Your spirits have always ignited me, sending me to
great heights and providing a deeper
understanding of humankind.

To all the people in the restaurant industry.
I know how challenging your work is and I applaud you.

To all the people who feel trapped in life, I offer this book to you,
knowing that Faith, Hope and Charity can change your situation.

Finally, I praise the Father, Son and Holy Spirit
who continuously inspire me to live life every day
for the highest good.

Acknowledgements

To my mother who taught me that honesty and hard work will always equal a good day's pay.

To my Aunt Jo who was breaking glass ceilings at Carson Pirie Scott & Co. before the term was ever created. Her love for me made me know that *Always* and *In All Ways* she believed in me, especially when no one else did.

To the people at the Hyatt Regency Hotel in Rosemont, Illinois, who provided a strict yet excellent learning ground for me in 12 years of waiting tables for them.

To Don Risser from Dawes Transport who hired me as a commissioned representative in 1986 and supported all my ideas and endeavors for many years.

To my first employee, Pam Troy, and all the loyal employees at New Age who never ever say enough is enough.

To Mark Graham, who listened to 48-hours of tapes and helped me deliver all of my views and thoughts into book format.

To Nick Galifianakis whose cartoons added great style and a sense of humor to the book.

To all my customers who believed in me, who encouraged me to follow my dreams, and remained loyal throughout my career.

To all our trucking companies; the true unsung heroes of this country. Without them New Age wouldn't exist.

To Charles and Sue Wells of Chauncey Park Press for putting all the pieces of this puzzle together for me.

And finally, to Loree Vick, who encouraged me to write this book and inspired me throughout the entire process.

Contents

Introduction

From Waitress to CEO

The greatest glory is not in never falling,
but in rising every time we fall.

I do not know if the sage who first spoke those words had my life in mind when he said them, but he might as well have. I have traveled a circuitous, implausible route on my way to my current station in life. I have tripped and stumbled more times than I can count. I was, at best, an average high school student. A college education was out of the question, not for a lack of smarts but a lack of motivation and money. I have the dubious honor of being a beauty school graduate who discovered she had no interest in plying the trade for which she had been trained, and who quit the industry less than one year later. Instead, I made a fine art out of waiting tables, a career I practiced for nearly 12 years. I raised seven remarkable children more or less single-handedly, and know now that few things in life come close to motherhood.

Today I am the owner and CEO of New Age Transportation, one of the fastest growing small businesses in America.

May I tell you that none of it would have been possible had God not opened one door after another for me? Yes, it was up to me to walk through those doors when they opened, and it was up to me to make the most of the skills I had been given along the way. I did that. But who would have thought that the skills I learned as a waitress would be the same ones I would apply in becoming a successful and savvy businesswoman; skills I rely upon every day.

I want you to know this: it matters not if you are flipping hamburgers at the local drive-through, slugging your way up the corporate ladder, or working 16 hours per day at your own fledgling company. If I can do it, you can do it; bottom line.

You will need four things to begin:
- A vision
- The desire for success
- A positive attitude
- An unflinching willingness to work your tail off.

The 12 simple principles that we will be discussing in the following chapters will help you realize your vision, turn your dream into a success, and make your hard work pay off. You will begin to understand that every step you have taken along the way and every job you have undertaken have been sources of learning.

This is what I have learned on my travels from a proud waitress to a proud CEO. And I know that similar miracles await you in your life.

Let the journey begin.

7

Chapter 1

Have Fun

Loving your job starts with loving your life. Showing gratitude for your place in the working world starts with an appreciation of the blessings God has bestowed on you.

Love what you do, and do what you love.

We have all heard these words before, or at least some variation of them. It is not a cliché, however. It is essential in the life of a successful entrepreneur.

Spending eight or ten hours a day being miserable at your job is not a path you are meant to follow. There is nothing more fruitless or more hopeless than waking up every morning and trudging off to a job or a work environment that has no appeal to you. This is not to suggest that your job of choice should be one with no downside. Every job in the world, no matter how satisfying, has its negative side. I was a waitress for 12 years, and faced plenty of turmoil and more than my fair share of difficult people. Despite that, I was still energized by it.

As a CEO and business owner, every day is marked by a never-ending stream of problem solving and decision making, some of them tough and some of them painful. It is not all pleasant, and it is rarely ideal. But I still can not wait to get to work every day. I can not wait to open our office and greet the employees I have grown to know and love. I never grow tired of the sounds of a busy warehouse churning with activity or the clamor of semi-trailer trucks loaded with freight and headed for destinations far and wide.

It is your life.
It is your story.
It is your choice.

With the exception of a brief, inauspicious stint as a beautician, I have had the good fortune of loving every job I ever had, from waiting tables in an exclusive restaurant high atop Chicago's Hyatt Hotel, to a sales position with no guaranteed income, and finally to my current situation managing 70 employees and a 100,000 square foot warehouse. The reason is simple. I discovered the fun factor in each situation. I went inside myself and came away determined to enjoy the work I was doing, the people I was interacting with, and the challenges they presented each and every day.

God has granted us all the ability to choose. It is an extraordinary gift. He has given us a free will and exercising that free will is one of the greatest skills I have ever cultivated. If I hoped to end the night at the Hyatt with $250 in my pocket, I had to make certain the salt and pepper shakers were filled. I had to deal with a bartender who might not have come to work in the best mood. I had to charm a chef who, like most chefs, thought the world revolved around him. Part of the fun was charming the chef, befriending the bartender, and making a game out of filling the salt and pepper shakers.

A CEO's life is littered with similar chores requiring a similar mindset. Lost shipments have to be traced, ineffective employees have to be dealt with, and disgruntled customers often require personal attention. I look at these situations as challenges, not obstacles; as opportunities, not annoyances.

I want my employees to exude the same enthusiasm that I do. I want them to feel the same pride I feel when a problem is solved creatively, or a new strategy is successfully implemented. I want them to feel the same sense of ownership I feel in a job well done. I want them to experience the fun in the job. Otherwise, what is the point?

The truth is, there are probably more negatively, than positively, motivated people in the world. But this is not a state of mind we were born with. We all have the ability to choose, so why not choose the positive approach? It works for me. And it can work for you. Guaranteed.

We are all imperfect human beings.
We are never going to be perfect.
That is not the point.
The point is
that we can and must be open
and receptive to the journey.

If my waitressing days taught me anything, it was that a big part of having fun in the workplace came from creating positive relationships with my co-workers. Reaching out to them, I discovered, was a reward in and of itself. Showing empathy was as gratifying as it was healing. Sharing laughter was a gift. Listening to their stories could be a source of extraordinary bonding, and I never tired of hearing people's stories. Where were they from? How had they ended up at the Hyatt in Chicago? What were their hopes and aspirations?

Taking an interest in other people should not be confused with manipulating them. Showing a genuine interest comes from the heart and makes the job more enjoyable for everyone. It is also good business. In the restaurant business, a friendly hostess would seat my section sooner. A cooperative bartender would give my drink order special attention. An obliging chef would give a little extra care to that table of six I was trying so hard to impress. Most importantly, this positive energy was bound to reflect in my interaction with my customers which naturally translated into more tips. Imagine that.

Having fun and discovering the joy go hand in hand.

These days if I walk into my warehouse with a genuine smile on my face, it is going to have a positive effect on my employees, which translates into positive interactions with our shippers and our carriers. If I make a point of remembering my staffs' birthdays or anniversaries, it cannot help but instill a sense of pride and community, which makes for a more efficient workforce and a more energized work environment. It is a win-win situation encompassing fun, enjoyment, and profit.

I try my hardest to wake up every morning with a positive outlook. I trust in God to help me through the tough times and to bless the good times. I have never been hindered by the prospect of failure. If you have faith, you can rest assured that all will turn out well, even if you do fail.

If ever my faith was tested, it was during my waitressing days. I was living hand-to-mouth. It was all I could do to pay the rent. I just hoped I had enough money in my pocket at the end of the day to buy food for my two kids.

But I believed then, as I do now, that the human spirit is powerful beyond words. I could choose to see the positive side of waiting tables, and I chose to milk as much fun from the experience as possible.

I know that waiting tables does not seem all that glamorous. Every night I faced an onslaught of strangers expecting me to be at my best and being at my best meant treating them like royalty. Every night I could expect to be on my feet for eight grueling hours wearing four-inch high heels and outfits better suited for a chorus line in Las Vegas.

It was up to me to determine how I was going to deal with this nightly soap opera. I could have fun with it. I could seek out the joy in every situation. I could laugh and share with my customers and my co-workers. If I did that, the night was filled with possibilities. The hours passed smoothly and with a minimum of drama. My customers were always more appreciative which meant my tips were always better. Mission accomplished.

I then took this same attitude and sense of fun into the world of sales. Eventually I made it the cornerstone of my own business.

It does not matter that I chose the freight industry. I could have been selling widgets. It is the attitude that counts. I now have 70 employees with 70 unique agendas. The one and only thing I know for certain is that I have the power to create an atmosphere that is fun and non-threatening. When I throw open the doors of our warehouse, I know I can take steps to ensure that every employee walks through those doors with a smile on his or her face and with the will to be productive.

We travel few paths in our lifetime that turn out exactly as we planned them. There are few bump-free roads in this life. We face relatively few tasks that do not have some inherent routine or boredom built into them. There are always chores that need doing. That is just life.

But, at the end of the day, these tasks and chores and occasional bumps are the things that make us who we are. The question is whether or not we can find the joy in these seemingly unpleasant or mundane endeavors. Can we really throw ourselves into them, determined to get the most out of the situation?

The answer is that we can, and we must.

So what happens when things do not go exactly as planned? We learn to acclimate. We learn to identify the joy and turn it into something fun. We choose not to be victims.

Waiting tables introduced me to a new breed of woman: the saleswoman. They would come into the restaurant carrying briefcases and wearing power suits with big shoulder pads and confident smiles. I would think, "I can do that."

So when the restaurant closed for remodeling, I took a grand leap of faith. I visited an employment agency and applied for one job after another. Inevitably, I was always either under-qualified or lacking experience. I was also a woman.

I never gave up. I never lost my will to fight.

I finally landed a job at $12.00 per hour as a customer service representative for a trucking firm in Elk Grove Village, just outside of Chicago. Customer service was not sales, but I decided to make the most of it. I realized the fun in the job came from the people I encountered every day. If I connected with them on a personal level, the days were more fulfilling. They would share their stories, and I could turn a situation that did not provide a tremendous amount of stimulation into something rewarding. I also believed without a doubt that I was on the road to something better.

To love what is, now and forever, is to live and rejoice in each moment along the way.

When my customer service job turned into a sales position, I knew I had found my niche. I was in my thirties, the fairy godmother was not coming, and I recognized this sales position as the "Big Door" that I had often heard of, this was my golden opportunity to shine. My love of the work drove me to greater heights and revealed ambitions that I had long harbored, but had never identified. No, it was not all a bed of roses, but I learned to face every day with a positive point of view and an overwhelming sense of gratitude.

I loved the work enough to start my own firm in 1989, and the success I have known with New Age Transportation is a byproduct of this love.

To this day, I love what I do and know I am doing what I love. A former waitress could not ask for anything more.

WELL, SOMEBODY IS IN THESE
DETAILS, AND I'M TOLD IT'S YOU.

Chapter 2

Pay Attention To Details

*It is either God or the devil in the details.
It all depends on how you want to look at things. I choose to
see God in the details.*

My company, New Age Transportation, was founded on one basic principle: special attention must be paid when it comes to our customers' needs and goals. This is a philosophy straight from my waitressing days.

Back then, the amount of tips I made over the course of a night was directly and irrevocably related to my ability to manage the details of every individual customer in my section. Attending to those details was more than crucial, it was my lifeblood.

This is no less true today. As a CEO, I might have 300 e-mails to read and respond to, three meetings to attend, and two conference calls to oversee all before noon. The details that arise from these

17

communiqués and these interactions can literally spell the difference between the success and failure of my company.

The same diligence applies to the people who work for me. The more invested and genuinely interested I am in the thoughts, ideas, and feelings of each individual employee, regardless of his or her position, the more dedicated they will be in listening to and acting on the needs of our customers. What could be more important?

You can bring the details to life by asking the right questions, probing a little deeper, and separating the chaff from the grain.

What I discovered during my waitressing days is that the world is made up of very unique individuals. I might have been serving a table of eight executives who had flown into Chicago for a high-level business meeting, all with one agenda and one goal. But when they took their seats at my table in the Hyatt, they were eight individuals with their own needs and wants. It was my job to accommodate each man or woman – to make certain each one had the right drink, a perfectly prepared meal, and just the right amount of attention.

A *Fortune 500* company or a three-truck shipping company is no different. Each is made up of unique individuals. The driver of the truck is one man; however, he represents his entire company. I have to treat him with respect, knowing I am putting my reputation on the line with his entire organization.

As true as this statement may be, it still requires a genuine interest in the product you are selling (food, freight, or financial advice), the customer you are serving (diner, shipper, or investor),

18

and the satisfaction of their needs. A cursory, I will-get-by attitude just will not do. This goes back to loving your job enough to give it your best.

The table of six at the Chicago Hyatt could judge my commitment to my job by the look on my face as easily as they could by my diligence in making sure their drink order was served without a hitch.

The head of any one of our most important accounts will know how much his business means to me by the punctual return of his phone call. He will also know by the punctuality of the trucks moving his rush order of freight across country during the middle of a holiday weekend. Details.

Still, we are just people. We are not perfect. We make mistakes. We forget sometimes.

A waitress forgets that a customer asked for brown rice instead of white rice, or a lime in his club soda rather than a lemon. A CEO forgets that the board meeting has been moved from 11:30 to 11:00 and her secretary forgot to remind her.

Sometimes all you can do is laugh.
And people can handle laughter a whole lot better than they can handle attitude.

It is not the end of the world. You have to let it go. You have to move on. What happened five minutes ago or five hours ago is water off a duck's back.

Attitude in the restaurant business had never been rewarded with tips. Back then my only concern when all was said and done for the night, were the tips in my pocket.

Attitude in the transportation business can have even more dire consequences. A shipper can change carriers with a simple phone call, and if I have done something to alienate him, he might just make that call.

I learned early on that I could change my attitude for the better by focusing on the details. I also learned that it was those details that helped me make the most effective connection with my client or customer.

Sincerity, in every case, is grist for the mill when it comes to details.

Not all details are the same, however. A drink order, a change in an entrée, or a request for more napkins are tangible details. You can write them down on a notepad if necessary. Intangible details such as, making eye contact with a customer, complimenting her outfit or his tie, or laughing at the bartender's jokes are just as important.

In the shipping business, I realized that asking a fellow executive about his granddaughter's soccer game was just as important as implementing his request for new shipping labels. I realized that acknowledging the innovative idea of one my employees in front of his or her peers was as effective as putting that idea into play.

Details.

If I were to compliment a customer at the restaurant on her "beautiful blouse" only because I wanted to remember that she was the one drinking decaf coffee, you can bet that my lack of sincerity would show through.

If, as a CEO, I call a shipper that we have been courting for six months and suggest that the purpose of my call is to check on his ailing health, then that had better be the truth. If I am really calling just to move our "deal" forward, he will know in a minute.

The man who said, "Sincerity is the way to heaven," also said, "There is no greater delight than to be conscious of sincerity." He was right on both counts.

One of the details that I found most telling and important to my work as a waitress was recognizing and honoring the personality of each table. The group that was out on a Saturday night, full of good cheer and laughter, often wanted me to be part of the festivities. If they wanted a waitress willing to join their "fun," then I did my best. A group of out-of-town businessmen might want a dose of good-natured flirtation. A couple on an intimate date might want a smile, timely service, and no more. The last thing the man with a book open on the table wanted was small talk. Whatever the mood, whatever the occasion, it was my job to make the dining experience a memorable one.

In my position as CEO of New Age Transportation, assessing the personality of my employees is much the same. Recognizing their individuality goes hand-in-hand with choosing the most effective mode for motivating them. Some people are introverted and need empathy. Some are outgoing and need validation. A manager who thinks on her feet is not necessarily more effective than the one who studies every nuance and checks every figure. It is up to me to acknowledge their styles and maximize their talents.

And that means paying attention to the details. It also means approaching my role with sincerity and commitment and knowing that the two are inseparable.

That commitment begins the moment I wake up. I start by giving thanks for another day (the most essential detail) and meaning it. The way I figure it, even a bad day is worth my gratitude. Then I turn my attention to the most important people in my life; my children. Of my magnificent seven, I have four living at home. Like any other single mother, my first task is to make sure they are up and dressed. Task number two is to fix them a breakfast with some nutritional value. Then I drop them off at school with a kiss and a hug. From there, I put on my CEO hat knowing that I have already had a successful day.

Be personable.
Why?
Because it is really all about building relationships.
The man or the woman with the big title is still a person.
They still enjoy it when I ask about their kids.
Do not be afraid to share a slice of your life.
Do not be afraid to get to know your clients as people.
Remember, it is relationships that put you over the top.

During my years in four-inch high heels and tawdry waitress outfits, I discovered that every person (i.e., customer, fellow waitress, chef, or busboy) was an individual who deserved to be treated as if they mattered.

So how do you make this seemingly obvious fact work for you? You listen to their stories, you take note of their human side, and you remember what makes them laugh and what makes them cry. You remember their husbands' first names and where they grew up. You take an interest in their dreams.

22

People do not forget a caring gesture. The rewards are personal, and as a bonus they can also become financial.

From my experience, there are no unimportant details. If a shipper tells us that their docks are closed for lunch from 11:00 to 1:00 and our truck shows up at 11:20, I have an unhappy customer on my hands. If we are serving lunch to a visiting executive from one of our important manufacturers, and his assistant tells us that he likes warm chicken on his salad, we see to it that his chicken is warm. Certainly, it is a matter of courtesy, but it is also good business.

As the head of my own company, I have to pay attention to every detail, and I also have to make sure that the people who report to me are doing the same. The old adage that you are only as good as the people who work for you applies to every business, regardless of size.

Paying attention to details starts at the top. So does caring.

A prime example of that is how at New Age Transportation we make a point of remembering the birthdays of every single one of our customers. We telephone the customer, put the call on the loud speaker throughout our facility, and we sing "Happy Birthday." It may not be the most beautiful rendition, but our customers love it.

We take the time to send sympathy cards whenever we hear about a death in the family of any of our colleagues or customers. Everyone at New Age Transportation signs the card, and it has special meaning because it is done with sincerity.

When my employees celebrate a birthday, I personalize a

card, enclose $50 and deliver it myself. Beyond that, each of their children receives a card with $20. I send their spouses anniversary cards. The money is nice, but the personalized note really seems to mean the most. I do it because I truly care. It may serve as an incentive to the employee, and that is fine. However, that is not the reason I make this gesture.

When I was a waitress, it often took an act of God to get in a word with the restaurant manager. When I offered a suggestion, I may as well have been talking to the wall. If I had a complaint, that was the last thing anyone wanted to hear.

At New Age Transportation, I have an open-door policy. Everyone is welcome. I value my employees' opinions, and they know I care about them as people. It is a win-win situation, proof positive that success really does hinge on the smallest of details.

Fate sometimes leads you down a road,
and you
have no idea where you are going.

In those cases,
my faith, my optimism,
my willingness to take risks,
and my hard work
has always been my saving grace.

ACTUALLY, PEA IS YOUR COLOR.

26

Chapter 3

Learn to Roll with the Punches

*I do not believe a person can be in business
and not have a spiritual side.
I believe you have to make a leap of faith
when things seem to go wrong and know that
better times are yet to come.*

Picture a typical dining night in the restaurant. I would arrive at 5:00 p.m. Before going on the floor, the manager would inform his entire waitstaff of the nightly special. That night it would be veal scaloppini and the chef had prepared 200 servings.

"So really sell it," he would say.

I always did. That night I made certain my description of the veal was tantalizing and mouthwatering. At 8:15 p.m. I was giving my pitch to a party of twelve, spicing it with accolades from previous diners and bringing smiles to everyone at the table. They all agreed. The special it was.

But, not so fast. I took my order to the kitchen and received the bad news. The chef only had two specials left. Sorry, kid. You're out of luck.

I had two options. I could go off the deep end, panic, and strangle the nearest busboy or I could roll with the punches.

I returned to my table of twelve very eager diners, delivered the news, and then sprang into recovery mode. I knew from experience that success depended on how I handled it.

I might say, "The bad news is that I only have two orders of the special left. The good news is that dessert is on me. Better yet, the next round is on me." Or, I might make a game out of it and say, "Okay, I only have two specials left as it turns out, so everyone pick a number between one and twelve." This was an old trick.

Then I would set out to make the prime rib or the house pasta sound even better than the special of the day.

The problem, in this case, might have been a shortage of specials, but it could just as easily have been a dissatisfied customer or a troublesome co-worker. It did not matter. An obstacle was an obstacle. A problem was a problem. If they were getting in the way of the tips I was earning, they had to be overcome or solved. In other words, roll with the punches.

Take the bartender—the bulk of his income came from the people sitting at the bar. How then was I going to make certain he did not ignore me? To begin with, I did not demand, I requested. I did not browbeat, I befriended. I did not slight him, I complimented him and I always offered my gratitude. Suddenly, I had an ally in my quest for bigger and better tips.

In 1982, my job at the Hyatt's rooftop restaurant was put on hold when the hotel decided to renovate. I hung in there, taking part-time jobs elsewhere and biding my time. The same Friday night I was supposed to return full-time to the Hyatt, a storm blew in from Lake Michigan and tore the roof off the building. No exaggeration.

When hard times hit, you get behind the steering wheel of your life and shift into drive."

I was a single mom with two children, and I had just been told that I would be out of work for another six weeks. This was more than a punch; this was a serious blow. But the lesson still applied. I had to make the most of it. I had to respond, to recover.

This simple twist of fate, as it turned out, changed my life. I did not panic. Nor did I opt for the first waitressing job that came around. No, something told me it was time for a change. So I walked into an employment agency the following Monday and completed an application. The sales job I sought wasn't available, but I did luck into a customer service position with a local trucking company. While it was not my dream job, it was a new beginning. I rolled with the punches. I kept my head high. I did not blame the Hyatt and I did not curse the weather. I took a bad situation and turned it into an opportunity.

That is one of the most powerful lessons I can ever share.

From the entry level position in customer service, I developed a passion for the trucking industry, and moved into sales, where my entrepreneurial spirit was born.

After seven years working for other companies, I started my own firm and in 1989 incorporated under the name of New Age Transportation. I saw nothing but good things ahead of me. I had three employees by this time. Suddenly, we were billing $100,000 a month. We set up shop in a beautiful, sun-filled office with a corner view.

Three years later, my biggest client pulled his account, completely without warning. In the blink of an eye, 40 percent of my business went out the window. I was devastated. I even cried. But only for awhile.

I turned to my faith. Less than one week later, after much prayerful consideration, I took the boldest step of my career. I changed the entire focus of my company from a commission-based operation to that of a broker, combining the logistics of transportation, distribution, and storage. This change was a risk to the financial structure of the company.

The strategy has been called everything from risky and perilous to ingenious and revolutionary. In my mind, I simply faced the reality of the situation in the most inspired way I could imagine.

Rolling with the punches is a daily part of any CEO's life. I may arrive at the office in the morning with a well thought-out plan and a relatively set schedule, but I cannot remember the last time a day went as planned. Strategies change, deals fall through, and negotiations take unexpected turns. Machinery goes awry, employees quit, and shippers go out of business, sometimes without warning.

On Labor Day of 2002, that is exactly what happened. Within twenty-four hours, Consolidated Freightways, one of the three largest trucking companies in the country, locked its doors and sent thousands of unsuspecting workers to the unemployment lines. Consolidated was one of New Age Transportation's most important carriers. It handled millions of dollars worth of freight for us every year. In the blink of an eye, hundreds of our customers were left in the lurch. Deserted terminals overflowed with freight. There were no drivers and no customer service people. Tuesday morning the phone lines at New Age were jammed with desperate customers. We had two choices: we could panic right along with everyone else, or we could roll with the punches. We chose the latter.

It is all about how you handle it in your head. That is what the people around you will see.

We rolled up our sleeves and got to work. With a barrage of late night phone calls and unflappable persistence, we convinced Consolidated Freightways' corporate office to release our customers' freight. Then we lined up replacement carriers, scheduled pick-ups, and routed deliveries. We did not stop until the job was done. Thanks to the efforts of my New Age Transportation team and our other trucking partners, we turned every shipment and made every delivery.

As the leader of my company, it is my job to adapt, refocus, and convince everyone around me that the world is not coming to an end, no matter what the crisis. If team members do not find responsive, calm leadership at the top, they will seek that environment elsewhere.

A missing shipment or a lost account is just like being out of the special of the day. You adjust. You sell the customer the prime rib; you buy them a drink. You track down your missing driver; you transfer the shipment to another truck. You roll with the punches.

Rolling with the punches is not something you can put in your Day-Timer, or on a time clock, because it seems the most challenging problems happen at the most inconvenient times.

I would often take the late shift at the restaurant because I was the only waitress who refused to leave early. I could not afford to and I also knew that late-night diners often turned out to be the best tippers. There were times, however, when the floodgates would open suddenly and the hostess would seat six tables in five minutes at exactly the same moment food for my two other tables was coming and someone across the restaurant was waving the dessert menu at me. What to do? Rule one: do not panic. Rule two: roll with it. I would ask a busboy to deliver my food and then pour water for my new arrivals. I would talk the hostess into taking that dessert order. Then I would take drink orders from three tables at a time. Smile at the bartender, nod at the chef, and make sure everyone knew how much I appreciated their efforts. Then swing by my other tables and see if everyone was happy with their food; see if my new arrivals were ready to order, and so on and so on.

Stress can be managed, and managed in a good way. If you are honest with people, it is amazing how understanding they can be.

One of New Age Transportation's most eccentric clients used to buy out-of-date mainframe computers from companies upgrading their systems or going out of business. He did not want the computers; he wanted the gold inside the computers.

One day, a driver we commissioned arrived at a pickup site and found the entire building abandoned. It was not his job to go up to the sixth floor and haul down several tons of equipment. It was ours. So we called up the building manager, stirred up some help from the local temp service, and got the ball rolling.

I do not allow my sales staff to complain about how tough the economy is, and I hate to hear them complain about how slow things are with their customers. If you have that attitude, you might as well close your doors. You can not sit on the pity pot too long.

Now the driver was behind schedule. In his haste, he forgot to brace the computers and check the lock on his rear door. It did not take much of a hill for the computers to shift, the door to pop open, and the computers to tumble out. A series of telephone calls eventually led to me, and by now it was 8:00 in the evening.

What to do? Roll with the punches. The first order of business was to send a message of calm. The second was to locate another truck, requisition a crew to help with the clean up, and hire a driver willing to drive all night. It was all doable. When the wheels were in motion, I called the client and shared the exciting turn of events. All he wanted to know was that the situation was well in hand, and it was.

We rarely get exactly what we ask for or exactly what we desire. But we have a choice when things do not hold true to our expectations. We can be victims, or we can be victors. The victim always feels as if he is receiving the short end of the stick. The victor does not hold anyone else responsible for his plight in life. The victor, as the saying goes, makes lemonade out of lemons.

An optimist never takes anything for granted. An optimist gets up every day and says, 'Well, thank God it is all working. We are a finely tuned machine, and we are going to get out there and we are going to make a difference in the world.'

The biggest complaint I remember hearing from my fellow waitresses back at the Hyatt was that the hostess was not seating diners in their sections. They did not see that it almost always balanced out by the end of the night; they only saw my four tables to their three. The problem was that this attitude often translated into poor service for those three tables. When this happened in my section, I vowed to turn those three tables into tips equal to, or greater than, the girl with four tables.

When I went into sales, I did not complain about the slow times. I refused to play the victim. I used the slow times to turn up the heat, to make even more cold calls, and to show potential clients that I would be there no matter what the economic climate.

Roll with the punches. Create an opportunity.

Chapter 4

Practice Patience: It Pays

God, let me be the best that I can be today.
I do not know where you want me to go, but wherever
it is, I am going.

I have always struggled with the fine line that separates patience from aggressiveness. And, as you may know, mastering one without understanding the other can be disastrous.

If you are too patient, the train may never come. You may let an opportunity slip past that might spell the difference between success and failure.

If you are too aggressive, you are likely to put people off. And once you have alienated a customer, client, co-worker, or employee, the chances of regaining their trust is small.

The waitressing trade was packed with lessons in treading this fine line. How often would my patience be stretched to the limit waiting for a hostess to seat my empty section? I often wanted to remind her that it is hard to make money if there are no hungry mouths to feed.

Every night there were occasions when I found myself patiently waiting; patiently waiting for the bartender to break away from one of his bar patrons to fill my drink order, patiently waiting for the man in the chef's hat to put my order up, patiently waiting for the cashier to run my customer's credit card, patiently waiting for a busboy to get his rear in gear and clean off my table so the hostess could seat another party. Though, more often than not, I would say, "Forget it. I am not waiting. Get me a tray. I will do it myself."

And, finally, patiently waiting for the couple that had come in at 5:30 to vacate their table before last call in hopes of turning it one more time.

I learned quickly that each person had the power to control my evening, and that pushing any one of them too hard only served to push me to the back of the line. No, these were not occasions for aggressiveness, belligerence, or impatience. These actions did not bring rewards.

When I turned my career aspirations to sales, and eventually to the creation of my own firm, I came to learn that my aggressive approach to soliciting business, and the aggressive attitude that helped me keep that business, only got me so far.

Sales is a people business, and most people rebel in the face of overly aggressive salespeople. They rebel, shut the door in your face, or slam the phone down in your ear.

There is that thin line again. Did you wait too long? Were you too patient? Is that the train of opportunity leaving the station without you? Did you come on too strong? Did you alienate the most important person in your life at that moment: the man or woman with the power to say, "Yes. You are the person we want to work with?"

A good dose of patience is not the same as saying, "I do not care."

As in: "I do not care if the hostess seats my section."

Or in the transportation business: "I do not care if the phone rings."

That is not what patience implies. But what it does imply is faith. I believe that if I demonstrate patience, the universe will reward me. I have never lost an account at New Age Transportation that in time was not replaced by another, and often one bigger and better.

Patience is not complacency.

Yet patience is more complex than that. Patience is knowing that I have all I truly need. Patience is believing that New Age Transportation has all it needs to succeed. It is knowing that my station at the restaurant will be filled. That is not complacency.

However, believing that I have all I truly need does not mean that I can sit back and do nothing. It means that I believe enough in my actions to know that the universe will reward me.

These may sound like difficult concepts, but to me they are vital both in life and business.

As a management tool, walking the thin line between patience and persistence can spell the difference between an effective leader and a failed one. Every customer is unique. Employees come in all shapes and sizes. And the most urgent situation may be the one that requires the most poise.

The restaurant business was highly competitive and this competition brought out the aggressive side of most people. One of the managers I worked with at the Hyatt was uncommonly strict and unforgiving when it came to mistakes. But what he did not realize was that most of the mistakes were the result of inexperience and insufficient training. He often showed a distinct lack of patience when it came to training his waitstaff, and he did not seem to understand that we were the face of the restaurant. What a catastrophic error in judgment!

When I started my own company, I discovered quickly that managing my employees required both patience and persistence. As much as I may have wanted every person I hired to mirror the qualities that I brought to the table, I understood that each was an individual with his or her own talents and his or her own personality. Each had a different learning style. My best course of action in getting the most out of them was to show patience in their development.

I also want the people at New Age Transportation to share my passion for the company, but I think it is one of my responsibilities to help nurture that passion. It does not necessarily happen overnight. But if I can give them a sense of ownership and pride in what they are doing, I know that the net effect on their lives will be equally as profound. It takes patience, but it pays.

Are there areas where I draw the line? Absolutely. I have no patience for people who do not care about themselves or their jobs. I have no tolerance for employees who do not respect their co-workers. And there is no place in my company for employees who do not understand that our customers are the most important people in their work day.

Why attitude over aptitude? Because it is far easier in my opinion to teach someone the ins and outs of the business than it is to teach a positive attitude, street sense, and commitment.

I can take the time to teach someone the logistics of transportation, distribution, and storages. Running a fork lift or a computer program are skills that people can acquire. For me, it is worth being patient with someone who might lack experience but who comes to work every day with positive energy.

I will take attitude over aptitude any day of the week.

Jenny, my director of operations, and my indispensable right hand, is a perfect example. She was twenty when I hired her as a nanny for two of my seven children. When Jenny gave her mom as one of her references, I knew I was onto something. Her work ethic, from day one, was nothing short of outstanding. She took charge of the kids without stepping on my toes, and they loved her. She took initiative around the house that went well beyond her duties as a nanny. She was diligent and conscientious. So when my kids were old enough to start school, I offered Jenny a part-time position at New Age Transportation. There was not one job she could not handle or a skill she was not willing to learn.

Unlike me, the consummate extrovert, Jenny was quiet and soft-spoken. I did not try to change her. We shared the same work ethic, and that was enough. I encouraged her to be vocal when necessary and aggressive when the situation required it. I did everything I could to inspire her self-confidence.

She eventually made herself indispensable to the company,

and I had to get a new nanny. The rest is history. I was patient, and it paid off. Today, Jenny and I are "Dynamic Duos" as noted on the cover of the Winter, 2005 issue of *Business Week's Small Biz Magazine*.

Patience can be a salesperson's best friend.

As a waitress, I learned early that it was far better to let my customers take their time with the menu, sip their drinks, and enjoy the Hyatt's rooftop view. I did not push for their orders. I would say, "No rush. Let me know if you have any questions. Relax and enjoy."

I do not believe in hiring from the outside. It rarely works. I believe in bringing people along slowly, showing patience, and promoting from the inside.

That was, after all, why they were there—to relax and enjoy—and the more enjoyable the evening and the more I contributed to it, the more generous they were. If they occupied my table for an extra half hour sipping coffee, I made sure their cups were filled.

On the other hand, if patience has a younger brother, it is tenacity. They go hand-in-hand. A show of patience, without the resilience to hang in there and never ever give up, is a dead end street.

I take a similar tact as the CEO of my own company. Years ago, when I was courting the business of one of the country's most important communications firms, I did not call once or twice, I called once a month for six months. I was not trying to be a nuisance. I just

42

wanted their business. And, once I had it, I promised to relieve them of their transportation woes forever.

A major cable company was even more of a challenge. When I was ready to throw my hands up and walk away, Pam, my executive assistant, never gave up. She showed the patience of a saint and the diligence of a true professional. The result was a million dollar account and one of the best working relationships we have.

We cannot put a time limit on our patience because every customer is as different as every waitress. Every potential shipper is as unique as every prospective carrier. Every situation requires a clear understanding of the circumstances. Tenacity is the ace in the hole. Tenacity makes it easier to be patient, but it also gets us moving when the time is right.

It is just as important to remember, however, that pressuring people is a huge turnoff. No one wants to be sold. A good waitress is no different than an effective salesman. You have to be accommodating and patient. But most of all, you have to make a customer or client feel as if they are the only person in the world that matters at that moment.

The message that patience conveys to a customer or a client is this: "I will be waiting for you, and I will wait all day if I have to. That is how much getting your business means to me."

It is all
in delivery.

YOU KNOW I'M ALWAYS HERE FOR YOU.

Chapter 5

Care About Others

I love you just because you are.

Every person—man, woman, or child—on the face of the earth wants someone to care about them. It is human nature.

Making the lives of others a little easier is our responsibility as human beings. It also happens to be good business. Caring about others is not a selective process. It is a code of conduct; a philosophy to be lived every day with every person we come in contact with.

Whether we are outgoing or reserved, gregarious or cautious, we all have the innate ability to reach out to others. I have always been a curious, caring person; traits which instantly became advantageous as I entered the working world. When I began waitressing, I discovered how powerful this gift of a caring nature was.

From my first day on the job, I found myself wanting to get to know my fellow workers, not because I thought I should, but because I enjoyed it. In doing so, I discovered that every waitress,

45

chef, busboy, and bartender had a story to share and a yearning for someone to hear it.

And while I admit that the stories I heard in my waitressing days were spicier and generally more compelling than the ones I hear in the world of transportation, they all serve the same purpose. A personal story opens a window in the heart of the storyteller, and by inviting you to peek inside, he or she believes that you genuinely do care about them.

As a waitress, the rewards were always twofold. I felt better about myself as a person and I enjoyed my work far more than if I had remained aloof or distant.

The Hyatt restaurant happened to be located next to one of the busiest airports in the world, and sometimes simply asking someone what brought them to Chicago was enough to show I cared. Intuition told me how much to probe and what types of questions fit which customers. On the other hand, I could show certain individuals I genuinely cared by *not* pushing conversation on them.

The key word in all these examples is "genuine." If my only goals in befriending the bartender or engaging a customer in conversation were simply self-serving, my insincerity would eventually show through.

People are not dumb. They can detect insincerity a mile away, and sincerity is the only thing that makes caring for others real. This is as true in the business world as it is in our personal lives. Not surprisingly, relationship building is not something we can do in a half-hearted fashion. It has to be sincere and with the best intentions.

The restaurant business attracts people from every walk of life, but there is something about the business that draws in people with the saddest stories and most difficult plights. There was always a busboy forced to support his family, or a single mother working evenings to make ends meet. Oftentimes, these were men and women who had hardened themselves against the world by erecting a protective shield. If I took the time to try and penetrate that shield, I often discovered that the busboy and the single mother truly wanted to share their stories, open up, and trust someone. They were no different than I was. They could be touched by compassion. And they were yearning for love, just like we all are.

> *We all have one common denominator between us; we all want one thing, and that is love.*

Fortunately, this willingness to reach out to others became a natural part of my role as a salesperson and eventually, as head of my own company. Caring was not just something I preached, it became part of the New Age Transportation culture. It began with my employees, first and foremost, and extended to our customers. It became and remains culture of actions, not merely words.

I try hard to practice what I preach. Following the tragedy of 9/11, when our men and women in the military were off to fight in Iraq, I instituted a program called "I Care." The concept grew out of a desire to support our troops in Iraq but feeling helpless to do so. We decided to do our part by creating a community of caring here at home for them to return to. The program encouraged our employees to reach out to different segments of the community in a constructive way, either by volunteering or mentoring. I think we all felt that if we could make even the smallest difference, it was worth the effort.

Another incentive-based program, "Character Counts,"

encouraged positive citizenship among our employees, authenticity in all our relationships, and a responsible approach to each other, our families, and the world around us. The program motivated our people to take pride in their actions and to teach by example. New Age employees were now helping carry groceries for older people and shoveling their neighbor's sidewalks and driveways. They were volunteering at their church and in their communities. They were taking notice of how they could help anyone, anywhere. The incentives, I discovered, took a backseat to the genuine, feel-good effects of caring. It reminded me of my waitressing days, when the simple act of reaching out could make all the difference in someone else's day.

This is not to say that everyone who steps through the door at New Age Transportation is familiar with this culture of caring. In the past, they may have thrown themselves into their jobs, but they may never have experienced a workplace that encouraged them to give of themselves in these ways.

It continues to be my job to reinforce with my employees that New Age Transportation is not just about self-gratification. We focus on family and community. I realize that if I can create a company of real people with real needs—needs that balance family security and a positive work environment with viable opportunity—then my employees will be willing to go the extra mile for me. They will embrace their co-workers as partners and friends, and they will do the same for our customers.

Looking back on my years as a CEO, I realize that it is not the product alone that has brought me to where I am today, nor is it the ebb and flow of the marketplace. It is the relationships I have built over the years.

If you look closely at the character traits that spell effective leadership, you will find a caring attitude high on the list which should come as no surprise. Of course, people are influenced by financial rewards, career advancement and other benefits but the number one reason cited for employee loyalty is the opportunity to feel good about one's job and to feel good about coming to work every day. They also want to feel appreciated, to know they are doing a good job, and to feel that the person at the top cares.

> *My goal is to create a work environment where every man and woman is able to grow and flourish as a person. My goal is to make every employee happy, because if they are happy, the customer will be happy.*

I cannot emphasize enough how dramatic the results of cultivating this deep loyalty can be. When my employees see how much I care for them, they suddenly view their jobs with more ownership and more responsibility. A New Age Transportation customer is suddenly "their" personal customer. That customer is a source of personal pride, and the service rendered them is a testament to our success as a company.

Mary (not her real name) is not the ideal manager. She does not really know how to connect with the people on her team, and she is not effective in a crisis situation. I would have trouble working for her, so I do not blame her team for having the same problem.

Mary's strength is an overwhelming capacity for caring. Every customer has special meaning to her, and she will stop at nothing to satisfy his or her needs.

Unfortunately, her yearly review reflected her lack of

leadership skills rather than her customer service acumen. When I read the report, I told my human resources director, "If I were Mary, this review would be devastating."

Yes, there were employees who managed their teams better and who performed faster and more efficiently, but they did not care as intensely as Mary did. So we changed her review to reflect more strongly on her caring attitude and took it upon ourselves as leaders to gently nurture her leadership skills. Over time, Mary grasped the leadership concepts and rose to the next level. A little extra caring worked for me, and it worked for Mary, too.

Caring is a two way street.

As much as I needed the tips I was bringing in during my waitressing days, there was always a voice in the back of my head reminding me that it was about more than just the money. And when I broke into sales back in the early 1990s, there were too many doors opening and miracles happening for me to miss the fact that there had to be a greater purpose.

I have come to realize that all that I have can be attributed directly to the grace of God. True grace is not something we come to expect or necessarily deserve, but true grace happens to those who believe, who are humble, and who are willing to give without expectations.

Then, as today, money remains only one outcome. Money is a residual that comes from God who taps me on the shoulder and says, "I want you to show people that the door of opportunity can open for them just like it did for you. I want you to show them how to see that door and how to walk through it. Your responsibility is to give them hope."

If you have the desire, want it badly enough, and are willing to work hard enough—whatever your dreams—good things will happen.

I also admit that caring about others is risky business. There are no guarantees that what you put into a relationship will come back to you. Risk takers make mistakes and sometimes they get hurt. That is part of caring too.

As the saying goes:
If the student has not learned,
the teacher has not taught.

Diane is a perfect example of a risk taken which paid off. I hired her straight from a low paying job working in an ink factory. At the time, she was a young wife and mother, with low self-esteem. She had lived in an apartment her entire life and felt that homeownership (let alone business success) were beyond her. Despite Diane's lack of confidence, she had a gift that I recognized: she cared more for others than she did for herself.

I took her onboard and my hunch paid off. Diane took to the transportation business like a fish to water and she is now swimming with the best of them. She has become a New Age leader and handles one of our most prestigious accounts. Everyone from the shipping department to senior management has grown to love and respect Diane. By the way, Diane is no longer swimming in a fishbowl. This successful career woman is a proud homeowner.

Caring has a ripple affect. It is contagious.
Once you have felt it, you want to reach out to others
and show them the power of caring.

51

I'M INCLINED TO STICK WITH THIS. I KINDA WANT TO SEE WHERE IT GOES.

Chapter 6

Stick With It

Be passionate. Never take anything for granted,
and never let the hard times drive you to your knees.

This was a typical scene at the restaurant high atop Chicago's Hyatt. It was 9:10 p.m. The dinner rush was finally over. Management gathered the waitstaff together and asked for volunteers willing to call it a night. I was always amazed at how quickly my fellow waitresses jumped at the chance. Not me. Never. I was a divorced mom with two sons and a thin wallet. I needed every penny I could muster just to pay the bills and keep milk in the refrigerator.

However, it was more than just desperation on my part; it was good business. I had learned that there was often more money to be made from late night diners and after-hour cocktail drinkers than there was during the so-called rush.

In a revolving restaurant, I would often run myself ragged

with 40 tables and a full bar. With the occasional convention letting out, or an unexpected delay at the airport…would I be willing to stay over? You bet I would. Was it worth sticking it out? Every time.

In my position as CEO of New Age Transportation, I learned quickly about the ebb and flow of our unpredictable industry. There are times when our warehouse feels like it is a mausoleum and we do not move a piece of freight all morning. And then, "Katie, bar the door." Fifty truckloads begin streaming in, and there is no way we have enough hands on board to handle it all.

This is the industry I chose, or perhaps it chose me. I cannot run off to the golf course just because the day starts out slowly, and I can not hide in the office when all hell breaks loose.

"Sticking with it" means being present in good times and bad, keeping a level head when it seems like all your hard work is going for naught, and pulling yourself up by your bootstraps when it seems the competition is passing you by. "Sticking with it" means believing in your dream so strongly that nothing can possibly deter you.

An enterprise of any size, or in any industry, requires total commitment.

You have to be on the job. You can not work part-time and expect to be a success. You can not simply pray for a miracle because faith without action is worthless.

You have to keep your doors open and your product lines shipshape through the leanest times as well as the boom times. Why? It is so simple and so obvious that we often just overlook it; you need to be there when the next customer walks through the door or calls on the telephone.

Through thick and thin, the message is the same: stick with it.

"Bring it on" was my motto when I came to work every night at the restaurant, and it has stayed with me every day since. "Bring it on." There were always waitresses who preferred a nice steady evening with three or four predictable tables. They would say, "Do not overload me and whatever you do, do not seat another soul in my section until someone else leaves." They were the first to complain if we were understaffed and the first to complain if the floodgates opened.

Bring it on.

Uncertainty is no reason to panic or fold your tent. Uncertainty is a reason for putting in extra hours and making those extra phone calls you have been putting off. Uncertainty leads to opportunity if you are just willing to stick it out.

The fact is that a willingness to stick with a project to the bitter end or to fight through failures manifests itself in a more vibrant work ethic. There is nothing more enjoyable than seeing seemingly insurmountable obstacles fall by the wayside because you wouldn't give up. The best part is that the result is almost always increased prosperity. These are the moments when you raise your arms in victory. These are the moments that make the hard times worth it.

If this sounds like the battle cry of an optimist, it is true. I am a complete and total optimist. In my heart of hearts, there is an unabashed feeling that I am not going to fail, no matter what I undertake.

This is not to say that I have not tasted failure because I often have. Given my background, how could I not? I have experienced failed relationships and my share of failed business ventures. But failure is just one more reason to stick with it. I am tenacious to a fault and that tenacity is a product of my optimism. I know things will turn out well if I just keep going.

I am a person who believes in my own ideas and I realize that an idea is just a seed that has to be nurtured. When I made the decision to move from waiting tables to sales, I knew the obstacles were tremendous. I had no experience, little education, and no male hormones. I was told hundreds of times that only men could succeed in sales and marketing, especially in the transportation industry. "You are a woman, so do not even think about it."

The only encouraging voice I heard was my own. I did not try to act like a man, instead I chose to rise above the gender issue and focus my energies on tackling the industry. I took advantage of the deregulation of the shipping industry that swept the country in the late 1980s and early 1990s. I carved out a niche that was too good for shippers to ignore and too lucrative for carriers not to embrace. The truckers and shippers did not care that it was a woman who was saving them money. They only wanted to know that I could deliver in the clutch. When I proved to them that I could, New Age Transportation became a household name in the shipping industry. No one stopped to question my gender or my education. They had seen my work ethic, my innovation, and my dedication to their needs. That is all a business partner or an employee wants. It does not matter what your trade is.

Someone once said that if you cannot take rejection, you should not go into sales. As true as this might be, it should also be said that rejection goes well beyond sales. Rejection is a huge part of life. I can not tell you how many times I walked away from a table at the Hyatt with a tip so small that I had to wonder what I had done to deserve such humiliation. I cannot tell you how many shippers I have called who have told me that I was wasting my time.

Be creative about rejection.

I know, for a fact, that the secret to selling new business is to get in front of people. I also know it does not just happen. You call and you keep calling. You call even when the frustration is almost too much to bear. You call and say, "I do not want to be a pest, but I want this opportunity. I want your business." You are polite and courteous – even when you do not want to be – and you follow up. And then you learn: it is the follow-up that seals the deal. It is sticking with it.

"I can make it happen" is not just a cliché or a mantra. It is part of my belief system. It is a way of thinking that I want all my employees to adopt. It is a winning attitude. I do not want my people focusing on their failures or their setbacks. I want them looking ahead while saying, "I can make it happen," and believing it.

One of the biggest blows I suffered in the early years of my business (this was back when we were still storing products in rented warehouse space) was the sudden loss of a major electronics firm, an account that represented almost half of my business. When I heard the news, I literally broke down and cried.

I could not understand it. I was convinced that everyone in that firm's shipping department appreciated the service we had been providing them. They told me so. I knew the competition could not beat our prices. What I did not realize at the time was that New Age Transportation had been caught up in the middle of a power struggle that had nothing to do with the quality of our work. Essentially, we had been thrown out with the bath water.

In the heat of the moment, no one cared that my business had just absorbed a potential knockout blow. It was a horrible time but when the shock wore off, I came out fighting. I made phone calls, wrote letters, and caught airplanes to both coasts. I consolidated my allies and tried to woo my detractors. All the while, we went after every new account I could think of. This was, in my eyes, the ultimate in sticking with it. Out of the turmoil, we emerged with a new business model, a new attitude, and new customers. Years later, we even won back the business of that once-lost electronics firm, Pioneer.

There is no doubt that rejection hurts, but it also opens doors of opportunity.

If the couple at table 26 stiffed me, I had a choice. I could dwell on it, stew about it, and let it affect the rest of my night or I could put it behind me and make the most of my next customers.

If a major shipper decides to relocate his businesss, I can look at the situation several different ways. I can panic and let my anxiety trickle down to my managers. I can go on the warpath and blame everyone in the office for letting the big one get away. Or, as is my option of choice, I can wish my old account well, get on the phone and track down every lead we have, and have faith that something just as good will come our way.

If there is one thing that the successful waitress and CEO have in common, they do not dwell on their losses. They concentrate instead on their wins. They dig in their heels and look ahead.

You can never rest on your laurels. There should always be something in the pipeline. You should always be planning your next big move or nurturing a new strategy.

Anything can happen to those who believe. Always remember that "good" is the enemy of "great."

If you are an entrepreneur,
always pay attention to your own
thoughts and how badly
you really want your business to
succeed.
And always, always keep going.

YOU'LL GET THE HANG OF IT.

60

Chapter 7

Join the Circus

A waitress is nothing if not a juggler extraordinaire.

From day one, a waitress either masters the various roles of a traveling circus, or she can look for a new occupation. The same rule of thumb can be applied to a CEO. She can be the juggler, tightrope walker, ringmaster, clown, or lion tamer.

As a waitress, the minute I stepped onto the restaurant floor I was spinning plates and walking that fine line between a successful night and a disastrous one.

In my four-inch heels and vaudevillian outfit I juggled people, personalities, situations, and subtleties as if my life depended on it. Every person presented me with a unique set of circumstances, and each had to be dealt with in his or her own way. The hostess with the flaky personality was one plate. The bartender with a broken heart was another.

I may have looked like I was trying to become the chef's best friend or trying to make the cashier laugh with a confidential story, but while juggling these and a dozen other "plates" over a six-hour shift, I had one ultimate goal: to go home with cash in my pocket and, hopefully, a lot of it.

A CEO's juggling act is no less complex or any less tenuous. My company's survival might well depend on how successfully I spin the many plates that seem to be piled on my desk every day.

Much like the waitress, I spend a good part of my waking hours juggling people and problems. Deals require negotiation. Carriers need reassurance. Shipments are damaged, lost, or late.

Every day I walk a thin tightrope that separates a demanding employer from an effective motivator. I do not mind listening with a sympathetic ear, but I will not tolerate excuses.

Truck drivers are a perfect example. They are, needless to say, indispensable to our business. Unfortunately, many of them lack the people skills of a Dale Carnegie graduate. If I need to pull out my lion tamer's whip, I do it diplomatically. If I have to use my ringmaster's bullhorn, I try speaking softly. Sure, I know I can always get them with a joke or two, and when I do it is just another plate spinning in the air.

> *Juggling is an art form.*
> *A ringmaster is only*
> *as effective as the people*
> *around her.*
> *A lion tamer is a master*
> *of subtleties. And I continue*
> *to perfect each and*
> *every one of these.*

Every person we hire at New Age Transportation comes fully equipped with his or her own baggage. Just like me. It is a balancing act making certain that individual baggage does not disrupt the flow of our operations. It is a delicate situation when personal baggage does disrupt things. If that plate gets away and smashes, you can spend hours putting the pieces back together.

Juggling can be fun, but it is also a lot of work.

Every time a customer calls, another plate starts spinning. Customers have needs, and satisfying their needs is what the circus is really all about. If you let that plate slip, you are out of business.

I have to admit that I relish my role as the ringmaster of the circus, and I know I have to pick my battles carefully. I have to know when the orchestra at my fingertips is in tune and when changes are necessary. All the while, I have to remind myself of the ultimate goal: to make a profit, yes, and more importantly, to make a difference.

It is like riding a bike.

When I first started my business, I set up an office in my home. The year I incorporated I became pregnant with my daughter Whitney. I was nine months pregnant on a very hot Sunday in August. I was uncomfortable, and anxious and decided to take a short walk. A short walk it was, because no sooner had I set out than I went into labor. I made it back home and immediately called the doctor. What ensued was a frenzy with me yelling, "Call the babysitter, get my suitcase, get the car." In the midst of it all, my business phone rang. Out of sheer instinct, I answered only to hear one of my customers insisting that he needed a flatbed truck for a pick up on Monday morning. I explained to him the personal chaos that was happening at the moment and his response was, "Does this mean you won't help me?" I realized then that no matter what was going on in my personal life, my customers would always need to know that they were being taken care of. By the way, my one employee, Pam, did move his freight the next morning.

A waitress learns the art of juggling by doing it every day. She learns how to handle stress, understands the ebb and flow that goes with peak hours and the inevitable downtime, and learns how to have a good time doing it.

When you have five tables demanding your attention, there is no time to say, "I cannot do it." You can, and you do. You juggle. You straddle the tightrope. You learn that honesty is the best policy.

You have to be in a position to react and to respond. I might go in on Monday morning and find out I lost my biggest account. It might have nothing to do with me. New accounts now become an even more vital part of the juggling act; you must have them. All the while, your focus has to be on maintaining the consistently high level of service your longstanding customers have the right to expect.

That is an important one: honesty. If you drop one of those spinning plates, either figuratively or literally, you are honest with your customer about it.

"I made a mistake on the special of the night. I thought we had three, but we only have one. Dessert is on me."

Or how about the CEO's worst nightmare? "Your shipment is lost somewhere between here and Pittsburgh. We are tracking it right now. Assuming it was not hijacked by aliens, (a touch of the clown) we will have word by morning."

Honesty and attentiveness go hand-in-hand. Every customer at the restaurant and every shipper at New Age Transportation want the same thing: 100 percent of your attention. You have to give them that attention without losing sight of half a dozen other spinning plates.

That is the trick. If you do not give a customer your full

attention, I can guarantee that you will overlook a detail that will surely come back to haunt you. Details that come back to haunt you inevitably cost you money.

A poorly cooked steak is the same as a misrouted shipment. I might not be directly responsible, but it is my plate that just tumbled to the floor. The hit to the pocketbook is mine.

Profitability might just be the biggest plate you are spinning. Without it, all the benefits generated by your company's success go straight out the window.

Everything in life is energy.

I mastered the arts of juggling and tightrope walking when I took a customer service job at a trucking firm in Elk Grove Village, Illinois, in 1982. I may have been optimistic about the opportunity, but I also continued waiting tables, just in case my new day job did not pan out.

I was working 75 hours per week. I was also raising two kids single-handedly and commuting from the freight office in Elk Grove Village to the O'Hare Airport restaurant during rush hour. It was a three-ring circus, and I was the main attraction. I had enough plates spinning in the air back then that I was not sure whether I was coming or going. All the while, I was urging my boss at the trucking firm to promote me from customer service and give me a shot at sales. I never gave up and never took no for an answer.

A year later, he gave me my sales opportunity. I never waited on another table again.

That is the way life is. We often find ourselves navigating unfamiliar roads. Personally, I always know that I can bank on my faith, my optimism, my willingness to take risks, and to work hard.

65

Oh, and I always know I can bank on my ability to juggle.

The circus, as chaotic as it is, is a family affair. In the CEO's perfect world, everyone is working with you, a team "performing" with the same goals in mind and the same positive attitude. This, unfortunately, is rarely the case. Part ringmaster, part acrobat, I have learned to juggle multiple personalities with nearly as many diverse work habits. The goal is to meld them all into a cohesive unit. The trick is knowing when to throw someone to the lions and when to give them a standing ovation.

Just when you think everything is going smoothly, a manufacturer calls on Friday at 4:00 p.m. with an urgent request to move two truckloads of freight from San Francisco, California to Richmond, Virginia; and they need it to be there by 10:00 a.m. the next morning. No problem. There is always room for one more spinning plate. Yes, the pallets are double-stacked, and all the boxes have to be numbered. Since a fully loaded truck capable of traveling from California to Virginia in 18 hours has not been invented yet, we hire a cargo plane. Of course, it is not as simple as loading and unloading the back of a plane. There is a refueling stop in Ohio and trucks that need scheduling in Baltimore. Finally there is a 150-mile trek to Richmond.

Always be a possibility thinker. Never say never.

Sure, it would be nice if we were able to drop everything else and throw all our energy into this one challenge. That, however, is not the shipping industry. There are still six other trucks to be loaded by the end of the day, a week's worth of billing to finish, an issue with an unlicensed truck, 40 employees leaving for the weekend, and…well, you get the picture.

66

So what do we do? We join the circus. We do not stop juggling until the job is done; lock, stock, and barrel.

I do not want my employees throwing up their hands in surrender. I want them to be possibility thinkers.

The circus is supposed to be fun. Enjoy yourself.

How can they juggle one more plate? It is all a matter of attitude.

True, not everyone can multi-task the way a juggler does. Some people are circus hands, some are clowns, some are acrobats. My job as ringmaster is to recognize their skills and maximize them. I am constantly reminding them of their roles as possibility thinkers. I tell them, "If you believe in yourself anything is possible".

Not that the circus ends there. Now it is time to go home and put on my favorite hat of all: Mom's hat.

Having a life away from the office is absolutely vital for everyone. I want my team at New Age Transportation to know that every juggler and tightrope walker needs to take a break once in awhile. Work is work; I want them to be the best they can be while they are on the job, and I want them all to have their own lives, too.

Take your weekend and forget the circus. Be a mother or a father. Remember your family. Go out on Friday night. Enjoy this beautiful world God has blessed us with. Have a life.

You have to honor the gift of your body.
You have to take care of your mind.
You have to renew your spirit.

67

LOSE THE BOW.

Chapter 8

Look Good to Feel Good

*We are a visual society, like it or not,
and we prefer dealing with well-groomed,
attractive people.
So, look the part.*

In the 1970s, every waitress who worked the Blue Max Room of the Hyatt Hotel was required to wear excruciatingly uncomfortable four-inch high heels and the most god awful red dress you can imagine. Not only was the dress red, it was a glaring red. It was cut mini-skirt short and decorated with ruffles across the rear end; truly Las Vegas material.

The outfit was a requirement of management. We did not have to like it, but we did have to wear it as if it was the latest fashion statement.

And it did not stop there. As a waitress, I did not go anywhere near the floor unless my makeup was flawless and my hair was perfectly styled.

69

As the fashion of the day, our outfits were deemed sexy, and our makeup was considered alluring. As tasteless as it might seem in retrospect, it was the image the Hyatt wanted to project, and the waitstaff was the face of the restaurant. Professionalism was the operative word. "Looking good" was not just a good thing, it was a mandatory thing.

Today, image and professionalism are mainstays in my ever-evolving business philosophy. Looking good to feel good is not only an article of faith I practice every day, it is one I try to instill in every one of my employees, no matter what their position is at New Age Transportation.

I do not want to imply that we look to hire Hollywood material at New Age Transportation. The beauty I am referring to comes from the inside out. The people we are most interested in working with have an inner strength that exudes confidence and kindness.

I have no doubt, however, that the man or woman who starts the day with an eye for dressing well will come to work with a more productive outlook than the employee who haphazardly throws on the first thing he or she grabs from the closet. I believe that the man or woman who makes a conscious effort with his or her personal grooming every morning is light years ahead of the ill-kept employee who may not even glance in the mirror before hurrying out the door. Looking good is a state of mind that permeates every facet of the day and enhances confidence. I know for a fact that the New Age Transportation employees who take pride in their daily appearance are those who care the most about their jobs and their responsibilities, and who take ownership of their place in the company.

However, looking good to feel good is not a beauty contest or a statement about body size. It is a personal statement that manifests itself in an individual's commitment. It says, "I am ready to give my all to an eight-hour day." Whether working in the warehouse or in the office it is important to portray professionalism—from the start of the day through to the end of the day.

Taking the time to look good and feel good always pays off. Investing in yourself is the best investment you will ever make.

My family, despite our disadvantaged financial status, always took pride in our appearance. Before the Marine Corps, my mother and aunt worked in the women's wear department at Carson Pirie Scott. My father spent 15 years doing data processing at Carson's. Every Christmas and every Easter without fail, my brothers, sisters, and I were rewarded with new holiday outfits. This was not a frivolous gesture of my parents; it was an essential part of our upbringing. The message was this: always look your best, always take pride in your own appearance, and try to associate with people who think the same way.

This prejudice toward appearance starts as far back as our infancy. It has been proven that newborns and toddlers gravitate toward more "attractive" people. We are aware at an early age that beauty is defined by ugliness, and human beings are drawn to beauty instinctively. No need to apologize for it. In fact, why not take advantage of it?

I know from experience that well-groomed, well-dressed sales people increase their odds of producing successful sales calls by one-half. A professional and polished first impression is priceless. It tells a potential client that you take pride in yourself, your product, and your company. More than that, it says, "I respect you as a customer enough to take the time to be presentable. You are worth it!"

Amazingly, audience perception of a public speaker is based ninety percent on non-verbal cues. It takes members of an audience approximately 30 seconds to decide whether they are going to listen to the speaker, and the biggest factor in making this decision is how the speaker looks. Do not believe for one second that sales is any different. Sloppy, poorly-groomed salespeople put themselves behind the eight ball from the get-go. In fact, you could say the same about almost any business that requires face-to-face contact with other people.

No, looking your best and making that strong, get-their-attention, first impression does not guarantee success. A waitress still has to deliver first class service. A CEO still has to produce a product worthy of her clients. But make no mistake the most important investment of time and attention you will ever make is the one you make in yourself, be it personal, psychological, or spiritual.

Presentation opens their eyes. The rest is content.

On the personal side of this equation are the clothes you choose to wear, the manner of your speech, and the confidence that allows you to look someone square in the eye and offer them a firm handshake. I cannot emphasize this enough.

If you do not feel confident choosing an appropriate wardrobe for your position, ask someone you trust for help. Spend a little extra without destroying your budget. Indulge yourself without going overboard. You will be rewarded in the end, believe me.

Girls, if you are not confident with your makeup, take a trip to your favorite cosmetic counter and get a makeover. Many places will do it for free. Ask questions. Allow them to give you hints. Splurge a little.

At New Age Transportation, we have an image consultant available to any employee looking for exactly that kind of guidance. She advises our staff on everything from appropriate dress, grooming and posture, to acceptable manners of speech, writing and business etiquette. Our consultant is completely upfront about appearance and presentation without being offensive. And that is so important. Her goals and mine are one and the same: to give every person at New Age Transportation the best chance for success by diminishing personal obstacles and enhancing natural assets.

You are what you wear.

I can tell you from experience that seeking advice is not a sign of insecurity or weakness. It is just another valuable tool meant to help you maximize your strengths and enhance your abilities. Seeking advice is not degrading, it is smart business.

If you do not feel comfortable about the clothes you are wearing or the words you are speaking, it is going to translate poorly to your customers. Sometimes you have to let go of old habits. Sometimes you have to be open to new ideas. Changing your image is not always easy, but, if success in the workplace is your goal, then I suggest you keep an open mind.

Dressing for success is about confidence. It is also about credibility. Credibility and appearance go hand-in-hand. I have seen it first hand, both as a waitress and as a CEO. Perception in the business world is not an illusion. People react to what they see and what they hear long before a waitress discusses the menu with them or a salesperson makes a presentation. If you are wearing a jacket with stains on it, that is what the customer will see and react to.

Whether you are a CEO, waitress, stockbroker, or schoolteacher, you are the representing partner for your company or organization, and it is your responsibility to look the part. As a CEO, I am much more impressed interviewing a man wearing a coat and tie than I am interviewing a man in khakis and a polo shirt. It sends a message that says, "You, your company, and this interview mean enough to me to dress the part."

We are, as I said at the beginning of this chapter, a visual society. We love to go with winners. Winners exude confidence. And while the right clothes may not mask all of our doubts and our insecurities (and we all have those), they do give us an outer confidence. When you look good, you feel good, and if you don't immediately, fake it until you feel it! You will.

My advice? You never have to apologize for dressing up. If there is a question of protocol, I always favor dressing up as opposed to dressing down.

Certainly we should always play to our audience. We should dress for the particular industry in which we are working. Every industry has its culture, to be sure, and honoring that culture is important. But that does not alter the rules. If you work in a warehouse, make sure your uniform is clean when you clock in. If you work in an office, make sure your shoes are polished. It goes a long way toward making an impression, and it also goes a long way toward elevating your confidence.

Sure, a dress code can be imposed by a company; wearing four-inch high heels was mandatory at the Blue Max Room of the Hyatt. However, I feel that a self-imposed dress code is even more important.

A self-imposed dress code says you
care enough about your job,
your company, and yourself
to look good.

POINTS FOR HONESTY?

Chapter 9

Honor Honesty

Honesty is more than just good policy,
it is a prized possession. It is an asset that serves as
a foundation for good business and even better people.

There are two ways of looking at the matter of honesty. An old saying puts it this way: "If you are going to be a liar, you had better have a great memory." This suggests that honesty is the best policy simply because your chances of getting caught are high. It is not worth the risk.

Another old saying looks at it differently, and is far less complicated: "Do the right thing." Unlike our first saying, this one suggests that honesty is the best policy because it is the honorable thing to do. This saying puts personal integrity at the head of the line, and it is hard to go wrong with that sort of thinking.

The problem with lying is that it chips away at the legacy

77

you are trying to build for yourself as a person. Every time you take a chip out of that legacy and sacrifice a piece of your integrity, it is almost impossible to build it back up again. Why is this? Because if you want to be trusted, you have to show yourself to be trustworthy. Not once or twice, but every time. Trust is about predictability and consistency, and it does not take much to put those two traits in doubt. A single demonstration of dishonesty is often all it takes.

Interestingly, we're often driven to lie because we do not think people can handle the truth. That is absolutely one hundred percent false. Take my word for it. People can handle the truth, no matter how bad the news is.

Not that they are always going to like what they hear.

For example, if one of my customers at the Hyatt ordered a filet mignon that came out of the kitchen cooked medium-well instead of medium-rare, I had two choices. I could try and put one over on them and hope they did not notice, or I could come straight out and say, "I am sorry, but we messed up your order. It is going to be a few more minutes, but I promise we will get it right this time."

They might be upset. In fact, they had a right to be upset. But at least they did not catch me in a lie. A lie would have put me in a hole I could not possibly have dug myself out of and the results would have been significant. For one thing, my tip would surely be minimal. For another thing, the customer might never have returned to the restaurant, and they might even share the incident with another potential customer.

As a CEO, if I know that a truck headed from Ohio to California is not going to arrive on time because the driver decided to stop in Las Vegas for a night of gambling, I have only one choice. I have to be honest about it with my client. Period. It does not matter that the client paid double for a non-stop trip or that his plant faces a shutdown if the product does not arrive on time. It is in his best interest to know the truth. He deserves the opportunity to plan his contingencies and to take whatever steps he needs to avert a disaster.

Whatever action he takes regarding my company is justified. But I can be assured of at least one thing: I know he is not going to hang up the phone wondering whether I have been truthful with him. I have been honest with him since the day he became a customer, and he knows that. I have earned his trust.

Honesty is not something you can practice with half the people, half the time. Whether you are an owner or an employee, you have to demonstrate honesty with your peers, with management, and with every member of the organization you work for.

For his part, he needs to know the truth and deserves nothing less.

For my part, I know I can look myself in the mirror when I get home and say without equivocation, "You did the right thing. Always and in all ways."

In the bigger picture, I know one day I will be judged on the strength of my actions, and the moment I am not upfront and truthful with the people around me is the moment I should get out of the business.

The restaurant business was a challenge to a person's sense

of honesty simply because there was so much money changing hands and so many people writing tickets and handling cash. The temptation to pad a ticket or add a dollar or two in gratuity to a credit card was enormous. But the benefit was never worth the consequences, and the proof was in the number of heads I saw roll due to such indiscretions. As easy as it seemed on the surface, I had to ask myself if the extra five or ten dollars was worth the risk to my job or the sacrifice of my personal pride. The answer was always "no."

Trying to gloss over a bad situation with a fib or a lie also goes against the grain of honoring honesty. Telling a customer his dinner will be out in five minutes when you know good and well it will be ten minutes only adds fuel to the fire. Be honest and tell him the truth: "The kitchen is behind. I am afraid it is going to be ten minutes at least. I am sorry. Can I get you another drink?"

Honoring honesty is always easier in the long run. It is one of life's truly ironic lessons.

Hedging the truth is hard work, and it is also bad business. It robs you of the energy you could be expending trying to make a buck elsewhere.

If it is true that 50 percent of all sales is emotion, then building a relationship grounded on honesty is a business philosophy every entrepreneur should adopt without fail. If it comes down to a potential client choosing between another transportation group and me, at the least I will have a record of trust and integrity on my side. It is a record I have spent my entire career establishing, and no one can take it away from me. You would be surprised how often a record like that tips the scales in your favor.

You can not build a record like that without consistency. All is takes is one lie for a person to lose faith in you. One lie, one fib, one exaggeration. If a truck is going to be at its destination at 5:00 p.m., I am not going to make a customer happier by telling them it will be there at 4:00 p.m.

The one and only way to ensure that my customers know I am telling them the truth is by telling them the truth every time. I never make an exception, and I never want my employees to make an exception.

That is the problem. Honesty does not allow for exceptions. If I have been upfront with a customer for five years and suddenly tell them the shipment will be on their docks and ready for the forklift one hour before it actually is, it does not matter how many times in the past I have been straight with them. One lie trumps a thousand truths; an ugly, but true, reality.

Remember this, too. A lie of omission is as damaging as a good, old-fashioned lie of commission. A customer, client, employee, or peer has a right to know the truth, and all the truth, about your dealings with them. If a shipper wants to know if I have ever had a problem with a certain carrier, it is not a wise policy to turn a blind eye on a past incident, no matter how long ago the problem occurred, nor is it fair to the client. Chances are good that they will find out anyway. Rather, it is better to use the incident as an example of a problem positively solved. I have not only been honest, but I have demonstrated my resourcefulness. Just like that, I have killed two birds with one stone.

In my waitressing days, I was dealing with food and with the people responsible for making that food taste delicious. A lot of things could go wrong, and I only had control over a certain slice of that pie. I could be cordial, efficient, accommodating, timely, and polite, but I could not guarantee a flawless martini or a perfectly prepared prime rib. I learned that trying to cover for people over whom I had no control, or trying to gloss over mistakes I was not responsible for, was not in my best interest. I was first and foremost responsible for the customers at my tables, and I learned to trust them with the truth. I might still pay the price for a bartender's watered-down martini or a chef's poorly cooked prime rib, but adding fuel to the fire by lying or hedging inevitably proved even more costly.

As a CEO, I can hire the best people and contract with the most reputable shippers, but I cannot be behind the wheel of every truck or make every sales call. Sometimes a truck goes astray or a salesman makes promises he cannot keep. I am responsible. It does not pay to make excuses for the driver or to blame the salesman. I am better off coming clean with the customer. If he or she knows they can count on me to give them the straight scoop, then we have a relationship based upon honesty and integrity.

Lying has a domino effect. Once one block falls, the rest are sure to tumble. Too often, one lie leads to another. The truth, on the other hand, stands on its own.

My employees deserve the same treatment. They deserve to know why I am making the decisions I am making. They deserve to be treated with respect even if we do not always agree. Playing games with people in the workplace always comes back to haunt you. The truth may hurt, but when the cards are on the table people at least know where they truly stand.

Honesty is its own reward. You not only avoid potentially disastrous situations or risk opening a can of worms you cannot control, but you miss out on the ultimate reward: trust.

At New Age Transportation, trust is our most valued asset. We take a client's prized possession—the product they work so hard to produce and the thing that stands between success and failure for them—and treat it as if it were our own. We do not just look at it as freight. It is our customer's lifeblood which means it is our lifeblood.

Always follow through.
And do not make promises you cannot keep.
You have to walk the walk.
When I get in front of
a potential customer, I say, 'You can trust that
we will take care of your account and handle your
freight as if it were our own, and you can
always in ALL WAYS trust that we
will be completely honest with you.'
My reputation has proven that they can believe me.

YOUR CONTRIBUTIONS TO OFFICE SCUTTLEBUTT HAVE FALLEN OFF THIS QUARTER.

Chapter 10

Mind Your Own Business

It takes a lot of energy to mind someone else's business.

If the waitress in the section next to me spent half of her night comparing my table of six to her three singles, the complaining wound up hurting her whole night because it took away from the energy and focus she should have been giving to her three singles. The net result was unsatisfactory service which translated into less tips in her pocket. Wasn't it the prospect of greater tips that led to all of her moaning in the first place?

Mind your own business, focus on the task at hand, and it will all work out for the best in the end. I guarantee it.

It takes extraordinary energy to invade other people's lives, especially at work. But there are always one or two individuals who cannot help stirring the pot. It's a professional compulsion. The more they stir the pot, the more they can fan the flames of discontent.

Then there is the person who thinks everything that happens, positive or negative, is going to adversely affect her. One waitress worries that another waitress has become too friendly with the chef, and therefore he is going to give more attention to the orders of that waitress. One salesperson has to know why his peer was put in charge of an account that he believes should have gone to him. Who cares? Mind your own business.

Sure, we're all curious. We all gossip from time to time. We all want to know why this person did this and why that person did that. It is part of human nature. But when does it become counter-productive or even destructive? At what point does business suffer? And worst of all, at what point are people hurt and their reputations damaged?

As a CEO, one of my responsibilities is the hiring and firing of office managers and salespeople. It is not my responsibility to explain my decisions to fifty of my employees. Yet, the amount of attention, interoffice cross talk, and emotion that firing an employee creates can sometimes equal a week's worth of productive work.

I like to remind them that people come and go, and that employee turnover is best taken in stride. I am not suggesting that people crawl into a shell or cover their ears, but I am suggesting that they stay away from matters that have nothing to do with them.

In my view, a CEO is much like the conductor of a symphony. Her employees are members of the orchestra who each play an integral part in creating beautiful music. If the conductor sees that one of the players is not practicing his music, or another is not taking the best care of her instrument, why would she allow that player to hinder a group effort that produces such melodic results? Why would the other musicians want that person in the orchestra? Most likely, they wouldn't. Do they need to know the dirty details? No. Mind your own business. Practice your music and worry about your own instrument.

At the Hyatt, there was always someone spreading rumors. There was always someone with a vendetta. There was always someone trying to figure out who was earning more, and who was seeing whom.

Devote your energy to areas of business that serve the company's best interest. In return, you will be serving your own best interest.

🙦

They were not helping to create more business or helping to enhance the Hyatt's image. If anything, their meddling hurt business by putting people on the defensive or driving them away. If anything, they disrupted the focus of people who really did care about the Hyatt's image.

When I left the restaurant business, I created a company that was in many ways unique to the transportation industry. I envisioned a working model based on third-party logistics that I firmly believed in and risked everything to bring it to life. My plan was to serve as a convenient, single point of contact for shipping, storage, distribution, and billing. It was a business model that hadn't been applied to the transportation industry before.

To this day, I make a point to focus on what we are doing and to not worry about what anyone else is doing. I try to anticipate change. I do not spend too much time studying what the competition is doing. Keeping up with the Jones' does not interest me. I have confidence in my company and what we are trying to accomplish and that is where I focus my energy. To do otherwise would be disastrous. I want my employees to have enough self-esteem to do the same. I also want them to trust me to know when the orchestra is in tune and hitting every note.

Do not be surprised to hear these two statements in the same sentence. They are remarkably compatible and speak directly to the point of minding your own business.

I want the people who work at New Age Transportation to be as proud of the company as I am, and I try to create a positive environment. I want them to defend our company if someone is verbally attacking us. I am also realistic enough to understand

Never say anything bad about a competitor and never bite the hand that feeds you.

that an employee may feel he or she has less of a vested interest in New Age Transportation than I do. But New Age Transportation is the company they work for, and the paycheck they receive every month puts food on their table and pays for their rent or mortgage just as it does mine. It is their lifeblood.

That lifeblood is something to be honored and respected. You may not like every single thing about your job, but the opportunity should be treasured. Talking negatively about your company, your peers, or your job may feel good after a couple of drinks with colleagues on a Friday night, but the good feeling tends to wear off come Monday morning. It inevitably generates negative energy in the workplace.

I also insist that my employees refrain from bad-mouthing our competition. As a matter of principle, they deserve better. Additionally, I do not want that kind of negative attitude infecting our company. If we stay positive, we will be more competitive. Period.

Gossip is the worst form of meddling...starting rumors and saying hurtful things. I do not participate in that, and I will not stand for it at work.

As a waitress, I learned how badly people wanted to share their story with someone who was willing to listen. I saw how people changed when I showed an interest in their life. A person's willingness to share their story with me was indeed a special gift. It was a show of trust.

Violating that trust is a serious offense. You not only expose that person; you lose them as a friend. It is a lesson worth learning. If you cannot hold your tongue, have the good sense not to pry or express false interest in the first place.

At New Age Transportation, if an employee has a problem with the company or a question about policy or procedure, I want them to have the courage and the professionalism to sit down with me and talk it out. I will always respect that approach. That employee has chosen the best avenue to express their concerns or vent their frustrations. I recognize leadership potential in this type of individual who is able to distinguish between petty gossip and constructive discussion.

Criticizing is another way we meddle in the affairs of others. We have all done it, and we have all been on the receiving end of it. Unless the criticism is truly constructive, it serves only one purpose: to stir the pot.

I believe that most people do the best they can. I believe that most people act on the information they have, and when they know more they act differently. When we know better, we do better. Simple.

If we know better, we do better.

We can all be teachers; each of us has knowledge and insight to share. At the same time, we can all be students and there is always so much to learn. Why waste our time criticizing when we could be instructing? Every person on earth has something to share, why not take the time to listen and learn from them?

Minding our own business might not come naturally to us, but it is a step toward being a better person, and it is also a step toward finding success in the business world. Make the effort. It is worth it.

I recently took my three youngest children (Jake, Luke, and Ava) to a marvelous exhibit at the Omni Max dedicated to sharks and their behavior. I was struck most of all by the fact that a dozen sharks will attack the prey of a single shark and fight to the death if necessary, even though there are hundreds of the same fish all around them. Why? Because it is their nature to desire what their fellow shark has.

90

Sadly, it seems to also be in our nature to crave what our fellow human beings have. We want their toys, their position, their wealth, even the lives they lead. Instead of being satisfied with the gifts we already have, we seem driven to want what we do not have and often cannot have.

A truly successful individual will appreciate what they have even while they are working to achieve more. They do not compare themselves to others. They mind their own affairs and they recognize the rewards that come from doing so.

Minding your own business is one of the truest forms of empowerment. The moment you focus your energy and attention on your own well-being, your own job, and your own challenges, is the moment you begin to grow as a person.

Always, always, always
honor yourself and your personal integrity.
And always, always, always associate with people
who think the same way.

I KNOW, BUT, ALL OF THE GOOD
IDENTITIES WERE TAKEN.

Chapter 11

Be Your Own Person

Before you can be your own person,
you have to discover the person you want to be.

A fully developed personality is not something we're born with. Yes, we come into this world with certain genetic traits pushing us in one direction or another, and, yes, our dispositions may display certain tendencies (i.e., a quick temper or a ready laugh). However, I believe that our personalities are meant to be developed over time, and that we have a great deal of control over that development. We have the ability to nurture elements of our personality. We can teach ourselves to adapt to a range of situations and relationships. We can change if we choose to. We can envision the person we want to be and we can become that person.

There was no better place to test this theory than in a restaurant filled with unique individuals with their own vision of a good dining experience. Some entered the restaurant seeking solitude. Some had business on their minds. Others were out for a good time, a few laughs, or a chance to party. Serious or romantic, rowdy or subdued, each wanted a waitress who reflected their mood. It was up to me to satisfy their needs while still being true to the real Carolyn. I found out I could do that, and do it well. More importantly, I learned that every person I met—customer, fellow waitperson, manager, chef, bartender, or cashier—gave me the opportunity to develop all of the many facets of my personality, allowing me to become the person I am today.

In my role as a CEO, I am aware of who I am as a person (a mother, a friend, a businesswoman). I realize that I have the ability to tap into all those aspects of my personality to adapt to the many situations I face every day, and to the many different people I encounter, as in the following:

We place such a strong emphasis on education, sports, and socialization with our children —all extremely important to be sure— that we often fail at the task of helping them develop their own special personalities. And they deserve that opportunity.

To the A-Type (the just-the-facts kind of guy), I respond as the Carolyn who prides herself on quick decisions, a sure grasp of the details, and a keen eye on organization.

A shipper who prefers small talk and a heavy dose of raw humor allows me to bring out the more gregarious side of my personality.

If an employee needs to discuss a problem with me and winds up telling the story of his life, he deserves a caring and compassionate ear. I know myself well enough to be that person.

I don't mean to imply that one needs to be an actor, playing a myriad of artificial roles. Rather each and every human interaction allows me to continuously grow and to discover even more about the person I am. It is remarkably fulfilling.

Maybe we expect the personality to develop of its own volition, and I suppose it does to an extent, but what we fail to realize is how much control we have over becoming the person we want to be. To say that an introvert is an introvert, no matter what, is only partially true. A person can develop extroverted skills. An introvert can learn to be outgoing when the occasion arises and even learn to like it.

To say that all waitresses and waiters are inherently extroverted would be false, but I never met a single successful waitperson who was not able to instantly display an extroverted flair when the occasion called for it.

It is important to understand our strengths and maximize them, and we must also recognize our weaknesses and take steps to minimize them.

Do not let anyone steal your power from you.

A serious person can teach himself to laugh more. An undisciplined person can teach herself to be more focused. A person who talks too much can learn to listen. An insecure person can discover the art of positive thinking if that is a trait he admires. Each of us can become the person we want to be. We can admire certain traits in others and emulate them. We can identify our faults and overcome them.

If I had listened to all the people who told me I could never

95

make it as a salesperson or a businesswoman I might still be earning the wages of a waitress. I might never have been comfortable having more than two children. I chose not to listen to them. Instead, I listened to my heart and my gut instincts. When uncertainty crept in (and do not kid yourself, uncertainty remains a real part of every single day), I put trust in myself and I put trust in God. I said, "This is the person I am. I am not the person those naysayers and doubters think I am." I have always been a believer in signs and now when people tell me, "It won't happen," I see God winking and saying to me, "You'll show them!"

Waitressing helped enhance some of the character traits that I already recognized in myself, but it also enabled me to develop qualities I was just becoming aware of. For example, I was always a hard worker, always willing to put in more effort and energy than the next person. And I was hardheaded enough never to take no for an answer.

Waitressing taught me to set my sights higher. It taught me to be proud of my circumstances no matter how tenuous they were or how uncertain. Waitressing taught me to have the confidence to deal with any type of person regardless of their position or personality. It taught me to trust my instincts and to believe in my intuition.

Every man, woman, and child on this planet has been blessed with his or her own spirit, and tapping into that spirit is the key to becoming a fulfilled individual. It allows you to grow and to change, to listen and to learn, and ultimately to take complete charge of your own life.

I believe in the spirit. I believe the spirit is continually inspiring me. I can hear a voice saying, "Go ahead. Do that. Try that. Take a chance."

You cannot run away from your past, and you cannot blame your past for your development as a person. Certainly, some of us have to fight harder than others to overcome the influences of our past. We take these mental images of our worst moments and revisit them over and over again. Do not do it. What is over is over and what is done is done.

Confidence allows you to become your own person, and becoming your own person builds your confidence.

Do not blame the past; forgive it. Take whatever positive learning you can from it and move on. Take control. Become the person you want to be.

I encourage every person reading these words to put yourself out there regardless of your age, your education, or where you see yourself in five years. Feel good about who you are. Develop your strengths, whatever they might be. Set your sights high as you envision the man or woman you want to be.

Every person has something unique and outstanding to bring to the party. Believing this to be true is the first step. Identify your special gifts. The next step is sharing them with the rest of the world.

In order to do that, you must surround yourself with positive people who also reflect the positive side of you. Accept their praise and their suggestions for growth. Take an honest look at your weaknesses and allow people to help you overcome them. Be a friend and you will have many friends. Accept yourself, and you will be accepted for who you are. Do not be satisfied until you see that person you are trying to be looking back at you in the mirror.

Part of being open and receptive to the journey in this search for the person we want to be is in recognizing both our strengths and our weaknesses.

One strength I honed as a waitress was my ability to relate to almost everyone I met (e.g., corporate heads or cab drivers, high-powered salespeople or newlyweds, chefs, bartenders, or dishwashers).

We are all on a great journey developing as human beings—not toward perfection, since we are all imperfect—but improving. Be open and receptive to the journey, and you will travel far.

I could relate to these persons no matter what their profession.

Today, I can relate as easily with the CEO of our largest account as I can talk to the forklift operator in the warehouse. It helps that I have lived both sides of the coin. But even as a waitress, I never felt either superior to the busboy or beneath the corporate types who used the Hyatt to negotiate million dollar deals. There has always been a comfort level that has nothing to do with those illusive boundaries created by position or money. The point is, I was aware of this strength and used it to my advantage.

Even though I may have lacked education, I have always been able to show my strong strength of character by willingly showing my vulnerabilities.

My recommendation? Be the kind of person you've always wanted to be, one who shows appreciation and gratitude. Do not fear rejection. Do not be afraid to go first. Do not be fearful of breaking the silence. Be a risk taker. Dare to be the person you want to be.

Diversity has always been a valued initiative at New Age Transportation, and I believe in it without exception. Diversity of spirit, character, and culture. I believe that every person has something to bring to the party. I believe in sharing the fruits of diversity, not hiding them away.

When you become all that you desire, you will have all that you desire.

I love the fact that every individual in our company brings to the table a lifetime of learned lessons and a host of diversity, whether it is racial, cultural, or socio-economical background. When you see it working, it is an awesome sight.

We do not judge people based on their minority status, we take full advantage of it. We allow the mix of people we have on board to push our creative juices and jumpstart our productivity.

We learn from different people with different stories. And we have fun doing it.

I do not hire people who mirror my personality.
I hire people who will bring out the best in me, people
who can stimulate me as much as I do them, and people
who are willing to grow with their jobs and
become the best that they can be.

Chapter 12

Expect a Miracle

My mantra has always been "Thank you, God".

In my early days working at the Chicago Hyatt, I was assigned to a nightclub on the second floor called The Blue Max Room. The club drew some of the top talent in the country. If Tina Turner or Joan Rivers was on the bill, we would be booked solid with reservations and I could expect a windfall in tips. On the other hand, if a lesser name or local act was the headliner, it was almost certain that my phone at home would ring and I would hear my manager say, "We can't use you tonight, Carolyn. We just didn't get the reservations we were hoping for."

I was the low person on the seniority totem pole which meant more often than not I was the odd man out. How was I supposed to pay my rent? How was I going to get food for my children? On nights like that I was reduced to praying for a miracle, literally.

Inevitably, my prayers would be answered in one form or another; that I can say truthfully. The next night a "high roller" might

101

come in, and his tip alone would balance the wages I had lost the night before. Or an unexpected convention might descend on the club and my pockets would be full for a week.

"Thank you, God!" I did not just say the words, I meant them.

As a CEO in an industry where account turnover is as fickle as a summer breeze, I have lost major clients with a day's notice. In most cases, it has absolutely nothing to do with how we are conducting our business. The fact is that companies move or merge or close their doors. There are always personnel changes. A new management team may feel compelled to bring in their own carriers. The reasons are endless, but the stress and anxiety are always the same. Big dollars are on the line as are people's jobs. Still, I have learned not to fret. I work harder. I trust my salespeople. I pray to God, and He *always* guides me. The new accounts we cultivate are oftentimes bigger and more profitable.

Refuse to be passive. Make it happen.

If I lose a top manager or a star salesperson, I know there is a reason. I tap my resources. I say my prayers. I have faith. And it often does happen that we find a wonderful, enterprising person who elevates our staff to a new level.

I expect a miracle and I am never disappointed. His Grace, large or small, is always close at hand and I am extremely grateful to Him.

"Thank you, God."

I believe in the manifestation of all positive things, including my own destiny and my own miracles. The key to this process is a sense of expectation. But expecting a miracle is not a passive activity. It calls for action, takes persistence, and requires faith.

There is nothing more effective in manifesting a miracle or steering your destiny than self-empowerment. If you put yourself in a position for good things to happen, they will.

At the same time, success without hard work rarely happens. I tell my children that they are responsible for creating their own success, and that, when they do so, the rewards are immeasurable. Yes, they can expect God to provide a helping hand, but only if they step up to the plate and make it happen.

I have an unlimited spiritual connection. I know that I am doing God's work, and there is no greater reward. Does this mean I do not have problems? Of course not. I still have to get up every morning. I still have to be a mother. I have to go to work. I have to deal with rejection. We all do.

In my days at the Hyatt, there were plenty of nights when I could have left for home once the rush was over. I never did. I knew all it took was one table of big spenders to double my take for the night, and I always believed that table would be seated before I left.

As a salesperson, I always believed that making one, two, or three more follow-up calls would bring me that new business I so desperately needed. I always believed I could turn a "no" into a "yes" if I hung in there. It is a matter of having confidence in myself and trusting in my God, and I can not think of a better team.

I can not do this alone. I need help. But this does not mean I am going to pray to God to bring me another million-dollar account. Yes, there may have been a time when I prayed for an abundant life and then threw in a quick reminder about the babysitter I was going to have to pay at the end of the night.

Now I am older and wiser and I believe God knows, without being told, exactly what we need. I believe that if I do my part, I can hand over the controls every once in a while and say, "What will happen, will happen." And I believe that if I have done my part—worked hard and offered a helping hand, while exuding positive energy—then good things will happen.

I believe in the power of prayer. I believe in the power of positive thinking.

There were plenty of nights when I left the restaurant with a meager $40 in my pocket. I would stop at the convenience store for milk, eggs, and cereal, and fork over anything I had left to the babysitter. But it was those nights, when I was hanging on by a thread, that made me appreciate a night when I walked away with $200 in my pocket.

Life is a matter of balance. We cannot know beauty if we haven't experienced ugliness. Failure gives perspective to success. A $40 night makes us appreciate the bounty of a $200 night. The loss of an important manufacturer reminds us to give thanks for all our loyal shippers.

When the competition outbids us for a job, I understand that God is saying, "This is better for you. It wouldn't have been a positive situation anyway." And I accept that. Certainly I am disappointed, but I am also accepting. Loss has always propelled me to greater heights. Loss brings out the fighter in me. I work harder. I expect more of myself, and I believe a miracle is just around the corner.

Every morning when I wake up, I have a conversation with God. I say, "Today, let me be everything you want me to be. How can I serve you today?"

Spirituality runs like a thread through my entire existence.

Before I go to bed at night, we talk again. I say, "Thank you for the day and all its blessings. Thank you for this beautiful, wonderful life you have given me."

These are prayers I adopted as a young woman, long before the waitress became a CEO. Success was not about money back then (even when I was counting tips down to the last nickel) and it is not about money today. It is about service.

This thread of spirituality is particularly strong in the workplace. Do not be surprised. Spirituality touches anyone who calls herself or himself an entrepreneur. Why? Because the entrepreneur values enthusiasm and intuition even above intelligence in driving them toward whatever quest they are pursuing. Enthusiasm is derived from the Greek word *Enthous*, which translates as "God within" or "Possessed by godliness." Intuition is our ability to perceive the truth, even if the facts do not support it, or if everyone around you thinks you are just a little bit crazy.

Remember, they laughed when the founders of Starbucks suggested selling a latte for $3.50. They rolled their eyes when some brave entrepreneur suggested selling bottled water for $2.00. Look what happened.

Trusting your intuition and letting your enthusiasm run wild is what drives the entrepreneurial spirit. Spirituality is a belief in oneself and in God. It makes the questionable seem possible, and the fanciful seem real.

Expecting a miracle is just as much about reaching out to others as it is about ourselves.

I expected a miracle when I was a waitress, and I continue to expect it as a CEO. Life is so much easier when you put your faith in God's hands, and so is work. Does that mean we approach life with any less gusto or work with any less energy? Of course not. It just means we have someone out there to share the load with us.

I started my "Expect a Miracle" Foundation in 2000 almost on a whim. One of our smaller customers was convicted of a crime and I found myself worrying about his children. What was to become of them now? The family had been left with a stack of unpaid bills and no father. These children were paying for the sins of their father. It did not seem right. I began dropping a few dollars in their mailbox to help pay for the "little extras," as I call them.

That simple philosophy is what the "Expect a Miracle" Foundation is based on. It helps single working parents to provide their kids with the "little extras"—small things that should be the right of any child.

We donate Christmas presents, prom tickets, karate lessons, swimming classes, sporting equipment, even dance lessons. I do not see this solely as charitable work. I see it as a means of teaching.

106

For example, I firmly believe that a child who is given a chance to participate in music lessons he or she never thought possible will be even more likely to reach out to others later in life. We owe the children of single-parent families every opportunity to express themselves and to grow to their full potential. We owe them every right to expect a miracle, and if a new baseball mitt or a chance to study theater moves them a step closer to pursuing their dreams, then it is a small price to pay. We owe it to the single working mothers and fathers who are raising our next generation of leaders. We need to embrace them, help them, and love them.

*God,
let me be the best that I can be today.
I do not know
where you want me to go,
but wherever it is, I am going.*

One last thought. There is no order to the 12 rules we have discussed in these pages. Together, they represent a way of thinking and a way of conducting our lives.

We talked in the beginning of the book about four essentials for succeeding in business as well as succeeding in life.

It begins with having a vision. A vision which is driven by a desire for success and a positive attitude.

And finally, the piece that brings it all to life is an unflinching willingness to work your tail off.

We talked about having fun and loving what you do. It's not worth doing if you don't. Remember that life is about having choices and writing your own story.

In Chapter 2, we looked at the importance of paying attention to the details, and I think this applies to every aspect of our lives, not just business. That's how we separate the chaff from the grain and find that diamond in the rough.

Remember that when you learn to roll with the punches, life becomes less serious and more fun. Everyone faces hard times. It's the way you handle the hard times that defines you as a person.

In Chapter 4, I encourage you to practice patience. Never in my life has this rule failed me. I ask God to let me be the best person I can be each and every day, and then I go out and try to make it a reality. You can too.

Caring about one another, the fifth of my principles, cannot be a part-time endeavor. The need for love is the common denominator that binds us all, even though sometimes it may hurt. We said that caring has a ripple effect, and nothing could be truer.

We discussed that in business and in life sometimes all you can do is stick with it. Believe in your passion and take nothing for granted. It's hard to go wrong if you're not willing to accept defeat, and if you believe that defeat is just another opportunity waiting to happen.

In Chapter 7, we talked about the necessity of "joining the circus." All this means is that life comes at us fast and sometimes we have to walk a tightrope and juggle at the same time. But this is no problem for a possibility thinker. It's what makes life so much fun.

Don't forget the principle of looking good to feel good. It pays off every time you step out the door. This is not a matter of vanity. This is about investing in yourself. This is about recognizing the power of presentation.

When we spoke about honoring honesty, our ninth principle, we talked about a priceless possession that is only of value if we practice it every minute of each day. And in the end, we discover that honesty is not only the right thing, it's the easy thing.

We began Chapter 10, Minding Your Own Business, by reminding ourselves that it takes a lot of energy to mind someone else's business, and I think that says it all. In the end, our own best interests are served, and no one gets hurt in the process.

Ultimately, it's about being your own person. Never devalue yourself and never stop believing in who you are. And finally, never ever let anyone steal your power.

I never leave a room or end an important conversation without reminding my friends and family to expect a miracle, and I would never end this book without doing that now.

Remember the power of positive thinking. Never forget to say, "Thank you, God."

Always, in All Ways: Expect a Miracle.

A Little About the Author . . . .

I am the product of our country's finest. My parents, Rose Murphy and Edward Rohr, were Marines. They met in the Corps during World War II where they enlisted because they both believed it attracted the highest caliber of men and women. If they were going to do their duty for their country, they would start at the top.

My mother was stationed at Great Lakes Naval Training Station in North Chicago, Illinois. My father was brought there after being stricken with malaria while serving in the Philippines. As fate would have it, their paths crossed and two months later, they married.

Devout Catholics, four children were born in five years. Two more followed in close pace. When the war ended, housing was tight for my parents as well as for all the men and women who were now ready to settle into family life. To ease the transition, the government developed quonset housing where hundreds of families lived until they could move on. That is where we lived for five years.

I was born the fourth of these six children. To understand me, one must understand the bloodline I was born into. My parents were humble and proud people, who took risks, dreamed big, and trusted God in the journey their beliefs would take them on.

My childhood years were challenged with financial turmoil. Simply put, there were too many children and not enough means to support them. To say we went without would be an understatement, even in those days and certainly by today's standards.

People have always asked me, "How, and when did you develop such a strong faith and belief in God?" I believe it started on Christmas morning, 1960. I was 9 years old and awoke on Christmas as I had in previous years pulling my siblings out of bed and running to discover the gifts under the tree. Normally we would have had to wake our parents, but oddly this year they were already up. My father was sitting in his favorite chair holding his rosary beads and praying. I remember so vividly seeing tears streaming down his face. I was young and so very unaware what was actually happening. My father had ulcers and he was hemorrhaging internally. I can only imagine the pain he was experiencing. I remember my mother pleading with him to call an ambulance and my dad saying, "Not yet, let the children open their gifts." Even as all six of us were caught up in the joyful moments of that morning, my father continued to pray the rosary for strength to get through the pain. When we finally finished opening our gifts, the ambulance came and took my father away. The doctor told us later it was a miracle that my father survived. My belief in the power of prayer was born that Christmas morning and remains a foundation of my life today.

Sadly, five years later, in 1965, my father died during surgery to remove the ulcers which had caused him such chronic pain. We were told it was a post surgical infection. In those days, no one sued. We just packed up his belongings and went home to make a life without him.

Left with six children between the ages of 6 and 19, my mother worked hard at her job, leaving at 6:00 a.m. and returning at 6:00 p.m. Overwhelming as it may have seemed, she taught us all the true meaning of hard work and perseverance. She did the best she could, and more.

111

We were all left to emotionally care for ourselves. I started working at Jewel Food stores at age 15. There was no car, so I had to walk two miles, or find a ride. I always felt the need to care for my younger siblings to fill the void that was left in our lives as a result of the death of our father. What once was chaos in our home was now an eerie silence. I was left to finish what was started and entered life and its responsibilities far too soon for a young girl.

My father had only one wish as a parent. He wanted his children to be a credit to society. I have always dedicated myself to making his wish come true. I know my mother is proud of me as well.